I0559663

Prepare for the interview –

Get the Job

By

Miguel Abrams

Copyright © **2025** *Miguel Abrams*

All rights reserved. No part of this book may be reproduced or distributed in any form without written permission from the author, except for brief quotations used in reviews or scholarly work. This is a work of nonfiction based on the author's experiences and professional insights.

ISBN:
978-1-966901-51-8 **eBook**
978-1-966901-49-5 **Paperback**
978-1-966901-50-1 **Hardback**

Printed in the *United States of America*

Acknowledgments

This book is more than just a guide—it is a reflection of the unwavering support, encouragement, and wisdom I have received from those closest to me.

To my wife, Diana—your love and belief in me have been my anchor. Through late nights, career ups and downs, and new challenges, your patience and unwavering faith have given me the strength to push forward.

To my daughter, Andrea—your curiosity, ambition, and determination remind me daily why preparation and perseverance matter. You inspire me to continue learning and growing, and I hope this book serves as a testament to the importance of resilience.

To my brother, Walter, and our mom—your guidance has shaped my journey in more ways than I can express. Your encouragement has been a steady force, offering wisdom during crossroads and reassurance in moments of uncertainty.

To the mentors who have guided me through career transitions, personal milestones, job hunts, and promotions—your insights, wisdom, and kindness have made a profound impact on my professional and personal journey. I am truly grateful for the time, knowledge, and friendship you have shared with me.

Thank you all for being an essential part of this journey. This book is a reflection of the lessons I have learned, the support I have received, and the resilience you have helped me cultivate.

Contents

Introduction

Why Interviews Make or Break Careers

Interviews are one of the few moments in life where a single conversation can change everything—your job, your income, your future. Yet most people go into them with less preparation than they'd give a 10-minute presentation.

In today's ultra-competitive market, a polished resume and a decent personality just aren't enough. You need a strategy, a mindset, and insider knowledge.

As of June 2025, the U.S. unemployment rate hovers around 4.1%, translating to over 6.8 million people actively seeking work. That number doesn't even account for the underemployed—those stuck in part-time roles or jobs that don't reflect their true skills and ambitions. At the same time, a single corporate-level job posting often attracts over 250 applicants.

With artificial intelligence now screening resumes and hiring timelines stretching into months, the interview stage has become more important—and more elusive—than ever before.

In short, if you make it to the interview, you're not one of 250. You're one of maybe 10. Maybe 5. Now it's your moment.

This book is here to make sure you are ready to *own that moment.*

But I also know how overwhelming interview prep can be. I've been there.

My Story: From Jobless to Offers in a Week

A few years ago, I found myself unemployed during a time of economic uncertainty. My industry had shifted overnight, and like many, I was caught off guard. I applied for dozens of roles, tailoring resumes, writing cover letters, and networking—and still, the rejections piled up.

Then I made a decision: I was going to treat the job search like a campaign. Not a desperate scramble, but a strategic effort. I broke down every piece of the interview process — research, communication, psychology, even body language. I read what hiring managers wrote on LinkedIn. I practiced responses aloud until they flowed. I watched videos of successful candidates and studied what made them shine.

Within two weeks, I had three job offers—one came the same day as the interview.

In addition to my own experience as a candidate, I've also interviewed hundreds of job seekers over the years, observing firsthand what distinguishes a memorable, hire-worthy response from one that gets quickly forgotten. This dual perspective—from both sides of the interview table—has shaped the strategies and insights you'll find in this book.

This book is the result of everything I learned from that process, combined with insights from hiring managers, recruiters, and career coaches. It's packed with practical strategies, but also mindset shifts and behind-the-scenes advice you won't find in standard interview books.

How to Use This Book

Each chapter offers guidance, real-world examples, and *actionable exercises* to help you apply what you learn. At the end of each chapter, you'll find:

- **Quick Reference Boxes** to summarize takeaways
- **Mini Challenges** to turn theory into practice
- **"Behind Closed Doors"** interviews with hiring professionals
- **Your Interview Coach** worksheets to reflect and personalize your prep

Whether you're reading cover to cover or jumping to the sections you need most, you'll walk away with a toolkit you can use not just for your next interview—but for every opportunity to come.

Chapter 1

Should I Do Research? (Yes. But Not the Way You Think.)

Let's get something out of the way: yes, you need to research the company. But you also need to *research yourself*—your values, your patterns, your goals—and how they match the role you're applying for. Because interviews are not just about getting the job. They are about knowing which job is *right for you*.

"The number one reason people fail interviews isn't lack of experience. It's lack of connection—to the company, to the mission, or to the person across the table." — *HR Executive, Healthcare Sector*

What You Think Research Is:

- Googling the company 30 minutes before the call
- Memorizing a few buzzwords from the company website
- Repeating the mission statement in your own words

What Research Should Be:

- Understanding the company's pain points and how you can solve them
- Reading about the CEO's most recent initiative and connecting it to your skills
- Finding a team member on LinkedIn and noting a shared interest or background

- Preparing a question that shows insight, not just curiosity

Where to Begin Start with the Company Website

- **Mission & Vision:** This gives you the company's "why." How does your work ethic or past experience tie into that vision?
- **Values & Culture:** Is this a culture of collaboration or competition? Remote or office-first? Do their stated values match your values and working style?
- **Product or Service:** Ask yourself: How does this company make money? What do customers love or hate about them?
- **Careers Page:** The tone here is often telling. Do they emphasize learning? Work-life balance? Innovation?
- **Recent Press Releases or Blog Posts:** Great for understanding what is *currently* important to them?

Social Media Sleuthing

- **LinkedIn:** Follow the company and key team members. Read their posts. Are they thought leaders or sales-driven?
- **Glassdoor:** Useful for trends, but take reviews with a grain of salt.
- **YouTube or Podcasts:** CEO interviews, team showcases, product demos.

"One candidate referenced a podcast I was on and asked a follow-up question about something I said. I hired him on the spot." — *Tech Startup Founder*

Researching the Hiring Manager

Here is where you can turn an interview into a *conversation.*

- **Look at their career trajectory.** What have they done that you admire or relate to?
- **Check for common ground.** Same university? Shared interest in volunteer work?
- **Identify their priorities.** Have they posted about innovation? DEI? Results? Tailor your examples accordingly.

Insider POV: Behind Closed Doors

"I once interviewed two equally qualified candidates. One came in saying, 'I read your article on sales culture—that resonated with me.' He got the job." — *Regional Sales Director*

Practice Challenge: The "Company Snapshot"

Pick one job you are applying to and create a simple one-page Company Snapshot.

1. Mission, values, or recent news that resonates with you
2. One major product or service the company offers
3. What you admire about the company culture

4. A potential challenge they may face in the next 6–12 months
5. How your experience or mindset could help address that challenge
6. Other relevant details

Use this snapshot as a *prep sheet* the night before your interview.

Quick Recap: Why Research Matters

- ✓ It helps you determine if this job is right for *you*
- ✓ It gives you better questions to ask the interviewer
- ✓ It allows you to speak their language—and show alignment
- ✓ It makes you *memorable* because most candidates won't do it

Your Interview Coach: Reflect

- ✓ What types of companies do you thrive in?
- ✓ What values are non-negotiable for you in a workplace?
- ✓ How do your experiences align with the mission of this company?
- ✓ What question could you ask that no one else will?

Write your answers down. These will shape the story you tell in your interview.

_____

_____

_____

_____

_____

_____

_____

_____

_____

_____

_____

_____

_____

_____

_____

_____

_____

_____

_____

_____

_____

_____

_____

_____

Chapter 2

Turning Experience into Interview Power

Now that you have researched the company and the hiring manager, it is time to turn the focus inward. You have got the context, but what about your own story? What makes you a strong candidate beyond just skills and qualifications?

Your next task is to look back at your career, accomplishments, and the lessons that have shaped you. But, this process is not just about listing job titles or responsibilities; it is about identifying **defining moments**—those key experiences that showcase your core strengths and how they align with the role you're seeking.

Defining Moments Matter

Your goal is to pull out the **most impactful stories** from your career. These stories will illustrate the skills, mindset, and qualities hiring managers are looking for. So how do you get started? Begin by reviewing key situations that shaped your professional journey, and organize them based on what the hiring manager values most.

Interactive Exercise: Your Professional Snapshot

Before we dive into the categories, grab a notebook or open a digital doc. Start by listing the key moments in your career. Focus on **situations** that require you to demonstrate a particular strength. These might include a challenging project, a time when you took initiative, or an instance where you led a team through adversity.

Action Challenge: Spend 15 minutes brainstorming and writing down **5-10 key moments** from your career. Think of situations that have defined you as a professional.

Do not worry about organizing them just yet—just capture the moments.

What Hiring Managers Are Looking For

The following categories help you identify the skills and qualities hiring managers look for. Use these prompts to jog your memory and connect your experiences to the job you are applying for. These traits often come up in interviews:

1. Leadership

- What situations have required you to lead a team or group?
- How did you lead?
- What was the result?
- What did you learn that will help you in future leadership roles?

Pro Insight: A hiring manager does not just want to hear about a time you "managed people." They want to hear how you *inspired*, *guided*, or *empowered* others to reach a goal.

2. Teamwork

- What moments have challenged you to work within a team?

- What was your role?
- How did you handle differences of opinion or conflict?
- What was the result?
- What did you learn about teamwork that can apply to future roles?

3. Strategic Thinking

- What decisions required you to think strategically?
- What was your thought process?
- What were the potential outcomes of your decisions?
- What was the result?
- What did you learn from this strategic thinking experience?

4. Planning and Organizing

- What situations required careful planning?
- How did you organize your tasks and prioritize?
- What was the outcome?
- What did you learn that you could apply to similar situations in the future?

5. Communication Skills

- What situations required you to communicate effectively?
- Who were you communicating with?
- What was the message you needed to convey?
- What was the result?
- What lessons have you learned about communication that you can apply going forward?

6. Handling Conflict

- What situations required you to resolve conflict?
- How did you approach the conflict?
- Was there pushback, and how did you handle it?
- Was the conflict resolved?
- What did you learn about conflict resolution that will help you in the future?

7. Taking Initiative

- What situations required you to take initiative?
- Why was it important for you to act decisively?
- What was the result of your actions?
- What lessons did you learn?

8. Self-Motivation

- What situations required you to stay motivated without external direction?
- What steps did you take to maintain your focus?
- What challenges did you face in staying motivated?
- What was the outcome?
- What did you learn about self-motivation that will help you in future challenges?

9. Time Management

- What situations required you to exercise strong time-management skills?
- What actions did you take to manage your time effectively?
- How did it help your performance and work outcomes?

- What was the result?
- What did you learn that will benefit your future work?

10. Measurable Accomplishments

- What tasks or situations required you to measure and track your progress?
- Do you have concrete data or reports that can support your achievements?
- How did you measure success, and how often?
- What was the outcome of your measurable accomplishments?
- What lessons can you apply to future tasks that involve tracking progress?

Interactive Exercise: Creating Your Situation Inventory

For each category above, select **one situation** from your list of key moments and provide a detailed response. This will form the basis of your *STAR* answers later on. Your goal is to have **at least 10-15 polished examples** that you can tailor to almost any interview question.

STAR Method: Answering Questions with Impact

Hiring managers love structure, and the **STAR method** is a great way to provide clear, concise, and compelling responses. It stands for:

S – Situation: Set the scene. What was the challenge or task?

T – Task: What were the specifics of what you needed to accomplish?

A – Action: What steps did you take? What strategies did you employ?

R – Result: What happened as a result of your actions?

Pro Tip: The STAR method ensures your answers are direct, structured, and impactful, leaving no room for rambling or veering off-topic.

Interactive Exercise: Build Your STAR Answer

Now that you've identified your key career moments, it's time to put them into a format that resonates with hiring managers. The STAR method—**Situation, Task, Action, Result**—helps your responses to be structured as interview questions in a clear and compelling way. In this exercise, you'll see how to bring your experience to life using this framework.

Let us explore two fresh examples from very different contexts to demonstrate how versatile and effective STAR answers can be.

Example 1: Leadership

Question: Tell me about a time when you had to lead a team through an unexpected challenge.

- **Situation**: "During my time as a supervisor of customer service at a logistics company, our software system crashed during peak season, right as we were processing a backlog of high-volume shipments."

- **Task**: "I was responsible for guiding my team through the crisis while ensuring customers remained informed and delivery timelines were managed."
- **Action**: "I immediately called a team huddle, delegated roles based on individual strengths, and implemented a temporary manual tracking system using shared spreadsheets. I also coordinated directly with IT and created customer communication templates to ensure consistency across the board."
- **Result**: "We managed to maintain 90% of delivery schedules with minimal disruption. Not only did customer satisfaction scores remain stable, but my team also received commendation from upper management for adaptability under pressure."
- **Lesson**: "This situation taught me that great leadership in a crisis is less about control and more about clarity, communication, and trust. I learned to remain calm, make swift decisions, and empower others."

Example 2: Conflict Resolution

Question: Can you describe a time when you had to mediate a conflict between colleagues?

- **Situation**: "While working in a cross-functional product team, two colleagues—one from engineering and one from marketing—were clashing over priorities for a new app feature rollout."

- **Task**: "As the project coordinator, it was my responsibility to ensure the project stayed on track without alienating either department."
- **Action**: "I scheduled a joint meeting where both parties could air concerns. Then, I facilitated a discussion that focused on shared goals rather than individual frustrations. I introduced a compromise: splitting the rollout into two phases so both user experience and technical feasibility were addressed."
- **Result**: "Tension eased, communication between the departments improved, and the phased rollout was completed ahead of schedule with positive user feedback."
- **Lesson**: "That experience reinforced that conflict often arises from misalignment, not malice. With the right framing and empathy, you can turn tension into collaboration."

Behind Closed Doors: Hiring Managers Weigh In

"A candidate once shared a story about resolving a team conflict that could have derailed a product launch. What impressed me was not just the result—it was how they communicated empathy, balance, and problem solving under pressure. That's the kind of leadership we need." — *Hiring Manager, Product Development*

Final Thought: STAR Power in Your Hands

Crafting your STAR stories is more than preparing for an interview—it is about **owning your narrative**.

With each example, you are not just proving your capability; you are showing your growth, self-awareness, and value. Keep refining your responses and make sure each one ends with a **lesson learned**—that is where your personal insight shines.

Take 15 minutes now to practice writing out two of your own STAR stories. Try choosing one example that highlights your **leadership** and one that demonstrates how you can handle **adversity or conflict**. When the interview comes, you will speak with the clarity and confidence that only preparation brings.

Your Interview Coach: Reflect

Take 15 minutes now to reflect on the STAR process:

- Do you have 3–5 strong examples for each key area?
- Can you tell them concisely without going off track?
- Are there situations where you could add a "Lesson Learned" to enhance your response using the full STAR-L method (Situation, Task, Action, Result, and Lesson)?

Write your answers down, and keep them handy. When the interview comes, you'll be ready to tackle any question with ease.

_____
_____
_____
_____
_____
_____
_____
_____
_____
_____
_____
_____
_____
_____
_____
_____
_____
_____
_____
_____
_____
_____
_____
_____

Chapter 3

Structuring Your Interview Responses for Success

By now, you should feel more confident about walking into the actual interview.

You have conducted thorough research, compiled a list of impactful situations from your career, and identified how your skills align with the role. You are ready to deliver a stellar performance. The next step is to **put everything together** in a structured and compelling way during the interview.

This chapter will prepare you in a way that no college course or internet video can. Implementing the strategy outlined here will give you a significant advantage over other candidates!

The Key Question to Ask

At some point during the interview, preferably at the beginning, you should ask a simple yet powerful question:

"What are the top two or three qualities or characteristics you are looking for in the person you will hire for this position?"

The answer you receive will set the tone for the rest of the interview process. This theme should remain consistent, whether you have one interview or seven!

Action Challenge

Ask this question in your next interview. Not only will it give you insight into the role's requirements, but it will also help you tailor your responses throughout the rest of the interview.

Aligning Your Answers with the Hiring Manager's Needs

Let us look at an example:

Suppose the hiring manager says they are looking for someone who:

- Works well with others.
- Is always learning and improving their skills.
- Can handle multiple projects simultaneously.

You should take note of these three key requirements and make them the central theme for the rest of the interview.

Every answer you give should reinforce how you meet and exceed these expectations.

Using the STAR-L Method to Your Advantage

Let us revisit the **STAR-L** method from Chapter 2 and apply it strategically in this context. When a hiring manager asks you about time management, use the STAR-L method while aligning your response with their stated priorities.

Example STAR-L Response:

- **Situation**: "Yes. At my last company, I was given a new assignment as Operations Manager for my region. This assignment was in addition to my regular responsibilities as a sales consultant. As you can see, I had to practice effective time management!"

- **Task**: "The new assignment required me to analyze and interpret monthly and quarterly reports to communicate regional and local sales numbers. I also had to maintain constant communication with leadership to keep them updated on the state of the business. Managing my time effectively was crucial."

- **Action**: "Fortunately, my experience managing teams and handling multiple tasks prepared me to take on this challenge. I structured my days to maximize client interaction while dedicating time to my new responsibilities during lunch breaks, on the train, and in the evenings when necessary."

- **Result**: "I am proud of my results—I exceeded my sales quotas while effectively performing the duties of Operations Manager. My boss and the leadership team were pleased with my ability to consistently communicate the information they needed."

- **Lesson**: "This experience pushed me to refine my time management and communication skills. I became more confident and effective in my role, which prepared me for greater responsibilities. I look forward to applying these skills at your company!"

Final Connection

To tie your response back to the hiring manager's specific needs, add:

"You mentioned that one of the key qualities you're looking for is someone who can handle multiple projects simultaneously. As you can see, my strong time management skills enable me to juggle multiple responsibilities effectively, making me an excellent fit for this role."

Consistency throughout the Interview Process

Continue this approach throughout the interview and any follow-up interviews. Imagine the impression you will make when, during the final round, you are still reinforcing the three key qualities the hiring manager emphasized! This will demonstrate that you truly listened and understood their needs.

Most people appreciate someone who listens carefully and provides solutions to their concerns. In this case, you are showing that you not only have the skills for the job but also understand how they contribute to the company's success.

You are demonstrating that hiring you will not only benefit your career but also make the manager's job easier and more successful.

The Key to a Successful Interview

Ultimately, your goal is to communicate that:

- You have the skills required to succeed.
- You are enthusiastic and motivated to do the job well.
- You will contribute to the company's overall success.
- You are a great fit for the team and organization.

With practice and confidence, you can effectively convey these points throughout the interview.

Benjamin Franklin once said, *"By failing to prepare, you are preparing to fail."*

This wisdom applies directly to your interview success. If you take the time to prepare, your confidence and knowledge will shine through. On the other hand, a lack of preparation will be just as obvious to the hiring manager. Choose to prepare, and you will position yourself as the standout candidate!

Use the space below to jot down your reflections, STAR-L examples, and key takeaways from this chapter.

Whether it is a brilliant response idea or a specific quality a hiring manager mentioned in your last interview, writing it down now will make it easier to recall when it counts.

_____

_____

_____

_____

_____

_____

_____

_____

_____

_____

_____

_____

_____

_____

_____

_____

_____

_____

_____

_____

_____

Chapter 4

Closing the Interview

One of the top reasons candidates fail to get hired is surprisingly simple: **they do not ask for the job**.

This was confirmed in a conversation I had with a hiring manager who's interviewed candidates for over two decades. When asked what separates the best candidates from the rest, he did not hesitate:

"If I'm stuck between two qualified people, I always go with the one who clearly asked for the job. It shows confidence, intention, and enthusiasm."

That insight stuck with me—and I've seen it proven repeatedly.

Why Closing Strong Matters

Closing the interview is your last chance to influence the decision. It is not just about summarizing what you have said— it is about **making a memorable final impression** that reinforces your value and eagerness. Many candidates leave interviews with a polite thank you and walk away... quietly.

Nevertheless, hiring managers remember the ones who close like pros.

How to Close the Interview with Confidence

Use this as a blueprint and tailor it to your style:

Example Closing Statement:

"Thank you for providing this opportunity to interview for this exciting position. I know you are considering other candidates who are stronger, but I genuinely believe I am the best person for this role.

You mentioned you are looking for someone who works well with others, is continuously learning, and can manage multiple projects at once. I hope I have shown you today that I excel in each of those areas.

Let me ask—do you feel confident that I would succeed in this position? If so, is there anything that would hold you back from offering me the job?"

Pro Tip: If it is not a final interview, pivot:

"I'd love to move forward in the process. Is there anything you need from me to support the next step in the interview process?"

Tailor Your Close to the Situation

Different roles and personalities call for different tones. You do not have to sound like a salesperson. You can be bold, or you can be thoughtful and sincere. The key is authenticity. Whichever approach you choose, practice it until it feels natural, not scripted.

The Importance of Asking Questions before You Leave

Asking thoughtful questions at the end of the interview is just as important as answering them well. It shows the interviewer that you are *engaged, enthusiastic, and serious about the opportunity.* Failing to ask questions can unintentionally communicate disinterest, passivity, or lack of preparation.

Remember: an interview is a two-way conversation. You are also evaluating whether this company, manager, and role are the right fit for you. Smart questions help you gather valuable insights—and they leave a final impression that you are invested in mutual success.

Here is why having questions prepared matters:

- It demonstrates genuine enthusiasm for the role and company.
- It shows you think critically about your career and the business.
- It allows you to assess whether the position and culture align with your goals.

Even if your interviewer covers many topics during your conversation, always have at least three well-thought-out questions ready.

Here are a few strong examples you can use or adapt:

- **"What are your short- and long-term goals for the department or business unit?"**

This question shows you are thinking about how you can contribute now—and grow with the team in the future.

- **"What is the biggest problem or opportunity that I could help solve for you if I am hired?"**
Hiring managers appreciate candidates who are ready to roll up their sleeves and make an impact.
- **"How would you describe the company culture?"**
Culture fit is critical. Understanding how teams collaborate, celebrate success, and handle challenges helps you gauge whether you will thrive there.

Pro Tip: Avoid asking questions that could easily be answered with a quick Google search (e.g., "What does your company do?") or that focus prematurely on salary and benefits unless prompted.

Behind Closed Doors: What Hiring Managers Really Think

"We can tell when someone's just going through the motions. But when a candidate says, 'I'd love to be a part of this team, and I hope I get that chance,' that sticks with you. You remember it. They want it. And I want people who want to be here." — *Hiring Manager, Financial Services*

What if You Don't Get the Offer?

Do not let disappointment derail your confidence. Some hiring decisions are out of your control—budgets shift, roles change, internal candidates emerge. What you *can* control is your grace and follow-through.

- Always thank your interviewer.
- Ask for feedback if appropriate.
- Send a thank-you email within 24 hours that reiterates your enthusiasm and highlights one specific point from your conversation.

"Worst Closes" I've Heard (And What to Say Instead)

- × "Okay, cool. I guess that's everything."
- × "Thanks… um, so… I'll just wait to hear from you, I guess."
- ✓ Instead: "This was a great conversation—thank you. I'm excited about the opportunity and I'm hopeful we'll get to work together."

Action Challenge: Your 3-Minute Close

Write and rehearse your own closing statement. Practice it aloud three times in front of a mirror or record yourself. Make sure it:

- Recaps your alignment with the role.
- Reaffirms your interest.
- Ends with a confident request to move forward.

Your Interview Coach: Notes & Reflections

Use this space to craft and revise your closing pitch. Jot down key phrases or reminders that help you deliver it authentically.

_____

_____

_____

_____

_____

_____

_____

_____

_____

_____

_____

_____

_____

_____

_____

_____

_____

_____

_____

_____

_____

_____

Chapter 5

The Power of the Thank-You Note

You have researched the company, prepared thoughtfully, delivered your strongest interview yet, and closed with confidence. But before you relax—there is one final step that can **tip the decision in your favor**: the thank-you note.

Too many job seekers skip this step, assuming the interview is the end of their influence. But **savvy candidates know** that the follow-up is an extension of the interview itself—a quiet, professional encore that speaks volumes about your character, enthusiasm, and attention to detail.

Why the Thank-You Note Still Matters (More Than Ever)

Even in today's fast-paced, digital-first job market, the thank-you note remains one of the most **underrated professional tools** in your arsenal. Why? Because so few people do it well—or at all.

Let us break down what a great thank-you note communicates:

- **Appreciation** – It shows respect for the interviewer's time and effort.
- **Interest** – It reinforces that you are still excited and invested.
- **Professionalism** – It demonstrates follow-through and polish.

- **Memory Hook** – It keeps you top of mind during the decision process.
- **Redemption** – Forgot to say something important? This is your second chance.

What Hiring Managers Really Think

"If someone can't send a simple thank-you, I assume they're not that interested. It is not just polite—it is predictive. People who follow through during the hiring process tend to follow through on the job." — Senior Talent Director, Tech Industry

"I once hired someone because of their thank-you note. It was not generic—it mentioned something we talked about, and even a book I had recommended. It showed me they listened, cared, and were proactive." — Creative Director, Marketing Agency

How to Write a Memorable Thank-You Note

A thank-you note does not need to be long—but it **must be intentional**. Here is a structure that works:

1. Start with a Genuine Thank You

Open warmly and thank them for the opportunity and their time. Be specific—mention the role and a detail from the conversation.

2. Reaffirm Your Interest

Let them know your excitement about the role has grown. Reference something meaningful from the interview that reinforced your desire to be part of the team.

3. Highlight Your Fit

Mention 1–2 strengths or experiences that align with the position. If they shared qualities they value, tie your background directly to those.

4. Add a Personal Touch

Reference a moment from the interview that stood out— something you laughed about, a shared interest, or a thoughtful insight they gave you.

5. End with Confidence and Action

Reiterate your interest and enthusiasm. Express hope for the next step, and offer to provide anything else they might need.

Sample Thank You Email

Subject: Thank You for the Interview – *[Your Name]*

Dear *[Interviewer's Name]*,

Thank you so much for taking the time to speak with me *[yesterday/today]* about the *[Job Title]* position at *[Company Name]*. I truly appreciated the opportunity to learn more about the role, the team, and your vision for the future of *[Company Name]*.

Our discussion about [insert topic] really resonated with me. It confirmed how aligned my background in [specific area] is with the goals you outlined, and it made me even more enthusiastic about the possibility of contributing to your team.

I especially appreciated your perspective on [mention personal insight they shared], and I have already begun exploring some of the ideas we discussed.

Please do not hesitate to reach out if I can provide additional information. I look forward to the next steps and hope for the opportunity to bring my experience and enthusiasm to [Company Name].

Warm regards,

[Your Name]

[Your Email]

[Your Phone Number]

[LinkedIn Profile – optional]

Thank-You Note Best Practices

- **Send within 24 hours** – Promptness shows enthusiasm.
- **Personalize each note** – Especially when interviewing with a panel.
- **Proofread** – One typo can undercut an otherwise strong impression.
- **Choose email over handwritten** – It is faster, traceable, and professional.

Mini Practice Challenge: Write Yours Now

Take 10 minutes to write a draft thank-you email for a recent or mock interview. Use the template, but **make it your own**:

- What key moment or takeaway would you include?
- Which of your strengths did the interviewer value most?
- How can you personalize the close?

This exercise will prepare you to hit send without hesitation when your next interview wraps.

Your Interview Coach: Notes & Reflections

Use this space to record key details you might include in future thank-you notes. Jot down names, insights, or personal touches that stood out during recent or upcoming interviews.

_____

_____

_____

_____

_____

_____

_____

_____

_____

_____

_____

_____

_____

_____

_____

_____

_____

_____

_____

_____

_____

_____

_____

Chapter 6

Bringing It All Together — Your Path to Interview Success

You have done the hard work.

- ✓ You have researched the company and hiring manager.
- ✓ You have prepared compelling STAR-L stories that spotlight your strengths.
- ✓ You have learned to align your answers with what hiring managers truly care about.
- ✓ You have confidently closed the interview—and followed up with a note that left a lasting impression.

Now it is time to bring all those pieces together and focus on the one thing that matters most: **execution.**

The Power of Preparation

Walking into an interview unprepared is like stepping onto a stage with no script. Even the most talented candidates falter without direction.

Preparation is what transforms anxiety into confidence and potential into performance. It is what separates the "almost" from the hired.

Here is what the most prepared candidates do every time:
Know the Company and the Hiring Manager

- Research beyond the homepage. Dive into recent news, product launches, and leadership changes.

- Use LinkedIn to learn about your interviewer's background—it gives you conversation depth and a chance to build rapport.

Analyze the Job Description

- Highlight keywords and skills. Know exactly what they are looking for so you can speak their language.
- Ask yourself: *"Where have I demonstrated this skill before?"*

Prepare Your STAR-L Stories

- For each core skill, have at least one STAR-L response.
- Practice aloud, record yourself, and revise based on clarity, confidence, and tone.

Nailing the Interview Conversation

The interview is not a test—it is a **dialogue**. And great dialogues happen when both parties are present, curious, and intentional.

Ask the Key Question Early:

"What are the top two or three qualities you're looking for in the person you hire for this role?"

This one question changes the game. It gives you the **answers** to the test before it begins—and allows you to tailor your responses for maximum relevance.

Stay Present and Adaptive

- Listen as much as you speak. Let the interviewer's tone and cues guide you.
- If a curveball question comes your way, take a breath. Structure your response. You are ready.

Close with Impact

- Reaffirm your interest. Ask for the job—or the next step—with professionalism and confidence.
- Do not leave them guessing. Let them know you are eager and prepared.

Following Up: The Final Touch

You might be done talking, but the conversation is not over.

A thoughtful thank-you note is your final handshake—an elegant close that sets you apart.

- ✓ Send it within 24 hours
- ✓ Personalize it with details from your conversation
- ✓ Reiterate how you'll solve their problem or contribute to their mission

"The best thank-you notes don't just say 'thanks'—they remind me why I wanted to talk to you in the first place."

— *VP of Talent, Tech Startup*

Interactive Exercise: Your Interview Readiness Score

Let us turn insight into action. Score yourself on the following:

Area	Score (1–5)
I researched the company and role deeply.	
I crafted 5–7 STAR-L responses.	
I practiced my delivery (aloud or recorded).	
I know how to ask the key "qualities" question.	
I have a strong closing statement ready.	
I understand how to follow up effectively.	

Total: _____ / 30

24–30: You are interview-ready. Time to shine.

18–23: You are close—focus on practice and polish.

Below 18: Revisit the core chapters. You have time to sharpen your edge.

Your Interview Coach: Notes & Reflections

Use the space below to write:

- Your personal "closing statement."
- A reminder of what matters most to *you* in a role.
- Any insights you have gained about your interview style.

(*Tip: These can also form the basis of your job acceptance decision.*)

The Winning Formula: Preparation + Confidence + Follow-Through

Success in interviews is not about luck. It is about clarity, connection, and consistency.

Prepared candidates:

- Communicate better.
- Think faster.
- Connect deeper.
- Leave stronger impressions.

By applying the strategies in this book, you have built a toolkit that will serve you not just in this job search—but also in every interview to come.

Final Thoughts: Keep Moving Forward

Every interview is a stepping-stone. Even the ones that do not result in offers prepare you for the one that will.

So whether you are:

- A new graduate entering the market,
- A professional making a career pivot,
- Or a leader aiming for the next level—

Own your story. Prepare like a pro. Interview with confidence.

Your dream job is not just a wish—it is a destination. *And you have the roadmap.*

7-Day Interview Prep Sprint (Bonus Resource)

To help you put it all into motion; we have included a 7-Day Interview Prep Plan at the back of the book (or as a free companion PDF). Use it to:

- ✓ Organize your prep timeline,
- ✓ Structure your STAR-L stories,
- ✓ Practice daily with intention.

Because preparation does not end when the chapter does—it begins when you decide to go after what you truly want.

7-Day Interview Prep Sprint: Your Fast-Track Plan to Interview Confidence

How to Use This Plan

Complete one focused task each day. Each activity builds on the previous one, culminating in a full mock interview and readiness check. You will walk away feeling interview-ready, with a customized toolkit and greater self-awareness.

Day 1: Know the Company Inside and Out

Goal: Research the company and hiring manager.

Checklist:

- Visit the company's website (focus on mission, values, news).
- Look up the company on LinkedIn, Glassdoor, and recent news.
- Review the job description and highlight keywords.
- Research your interviewer (LinkedIn, articles, public talks).

Reflection Prompt:

- What excites me about this company?
- What challenge are they trying to solve with this role?

_____

_____

_____

_____

_____

_____

_____

_____

_____

_____

_____

Day 2: Decode the Role

Goal: Understand the job requirements and map them to your skills.

Checklist:

- Identify the 5 most important qualifications from the job post.
- Match each with a personal strength or experience.
- Write down your "value statement" (why you are a great fit).

Quick Template

"Based on what I've read and researched, I believe this role requires someone who can [insert 3 traits]. Here's how I bring that to the table…"

_____

_____

_____

_____

_____

_____

_____

_____

_____

_____

_____

Day 3: Build Your STAR-L Library

Goal: Draft strong STAR-L responses for common competencies.

Checklist:

- Write one STAR-L story for each of these themes:
    - Leadership
    - Teamwork
    - Problem-solving
    - Time management
    - Initiative
- Use the STAR-L framework:
    - Situation
    - Task
    - Action
    - Result
    - Lesson

Reflection Prompt:

- Which story feels strongest? Which one needs refinement?

_____

_____

_____

_____

_____

_____

_____

Day 4: Practice Out Loud

Goal: Practice your delivery and polish your responses.

Checklist:

- Choose 3 STAR-L answers to practice aloud.
- Record yourself (voice or video) and play it back.
- Time your responses (aim for 1–2 minutes each).
- Note filler words, nervous habits, or unclear parts.

Coaching Tip:

You don't have to memorize your answers—just know the beats of your story.

_____

_____

_____

_____

_____

_____

_____

_____

_____

_____

_____

_____

_____

_____

Day 5: Prepare Your Opening and Closing

Goal: Create a memorable first impression—and a strong final ask.

Checklist:

- Practice your answer to: "Tell me about yourself."
- Draft a strong closing statement that:
    - Reaffirms your interest
    - Summarizes your fit
    - Asks for the job or next step
- Rehearse both until they feel conversational.

Reflection Prompt:

- Does your opening tell your story with purpose?
- Does your closing feel confident and authentic?

_____

_____

_____

_____

_____

_____

_____

_____

_____

_____

_____

_____

Day 6: Mock Interview Challenge

Goal: Simulate a real interview and get feedback.

Checklist:

- Ask a friend, mentor, or use an AI tool to roleplay a mock interview.
- Include behavioral questions and curveballs (e.g., "What's your weakness?").
- End the mock interview with your closing statement.

Reflection Prompt:

- What went well?
- What will you change next time?

Day 7: Final Touches & Thank-You Note Prep

Goal: Prepare your thank-you strategy and finalize your toolkit.

Checklist:

- Create a thank-you note template you can quickly customize.
- List 2–3 details you would mention from a typical interview.
- Prepare your interview day checklist:
    - Resume copies
    - Notes on company/interviewer
    - Portfolio or examples (if needed)
    - Outfit ready

Reflection Prompt:

- Do I feel prepared to walk into an interview tomorrow?
- What is one affirmation I will repeat before the interview begins?

Affirmation Example

"I've done the work. I belong in the room. I am ready to succeed."

_____

_____

_____

_____

_____

_____

You Did It! What is Next?

You now have:

- ✓ Deep company insight
- ✓ 5+ STAR-L stories
- ✓ Strong open and close
- ✓ Mock interview experience
- ✓ A thank-you note strategy

Whether your next interview is tomorrow or three weeks from now, *you are no longer guessing—you are prepared.*

Revisit this sprint anytime you want to refresh your confidence, sharpen your messaging, or refocus your strategy.

_____

_____

_____

_____

_____

_____

_____

_____

_____

_____

_____

_____

_____

_____

GOOD LUCK!

www.ingramcontent.com/pod-product-compliance
Lightning Source LLC
Chambersburg PA
CBHW051242120626
46547CB00014B/1752